PAUL HUDGINS

11/11/97

The Illustrated HORSE

The Illustrated
HORSE

Tom Howard

CHARTWELL
BOOKS, INC.

Published by
Chartwell Books, Inc.
A Division of Book Sales, Inc.
Raritan Center
114 Northfield Avenue
Edison, NJ 08818
USA

Copyright © 1994 Regency House Publishing Limited

Published 1994

ISBN 0-7858-0180-4

Printed in Italy

© Tom Howard 1994
The right of Tom Howard to be identified as the author
of this work has been asserted by him in accordance with
the Copyright, Designs and Patents Act 1988

FRONT COVER
Whistlejacket
by George Stubbs (1724-1806).

BACK COVER
by Théodore Gericault (1791-1824

PAGE 2
Sir Galahad
by George Frederick Watts (1817-1904)

PAGE 3
Horse and Rider
by Elizabeth Frink (1930-1993)

RIGHT
Sir Isumbras at the Ford
by Sir John Everett Millais (1826-1896)

Contents

Introduction

The horse appears at the very beginning of the history of art, painted on the walls of caves by our prehistoric forebears. As a symbol of power, a way of adding importance to a human figure, a record of a favourite mount or as part of a general scene, it appears in the art of every land where horses have been known. It is seen in early Mesopotamian and Egyptian art pulling a chariot, in both war and sport. The first known image of a rider on a horse – a boy bareback on his mount – is carved on a relief from Memphis (now in Bologna). Huge rock carvings of a mounted king found near Persepolis show how the physical elevation of the rider can emphasize status. This ploy was never more tellingly applied than by Anthony Van Dyck in painting the diminutive King Charles I of England on horseback and by Jacques David in his dramatic and glamorized equestrian portrait of Napoleon crossing the Alps. Similarly, a statue of a standing man is never so imposing as that of figure mounted on a horse.

The Persians were an especially equestrian people, and later Persian painting includes many fine natural studies of horses out hunting and hawking, being groomed or relaxing. Chinese painters, too, depict the horse with great naturalness that must be based on close observation. However, it would be invidious to single out any 'best' horse artists. From Phidias's carvings on the frieze of the Parthenon in Athens to the racing pictures of Toulouse-Lautrec, artists have captured the grace, spirit and strength of horses. One name does, perhaps, deserve special mention: the English painter George Stubbs, who has been hailed as 'Master of the Horse' He specialized to a considerable extent in horse paintings and made a detailed study of the horse's anatomy, although he was also a fine painter of other animals. One problem all painters had was showing horses at the gallop, for, until Eadward Muybridge took his sequential photographs of movement in 1877, no one was certain of the exact co-ordination and movement of the galloping horse's legs.

Many representations of the horse form part of historical paintings recording battles, processions and meetings between great men. The working horse can be found in Roman mosaics and medieval illumination, as

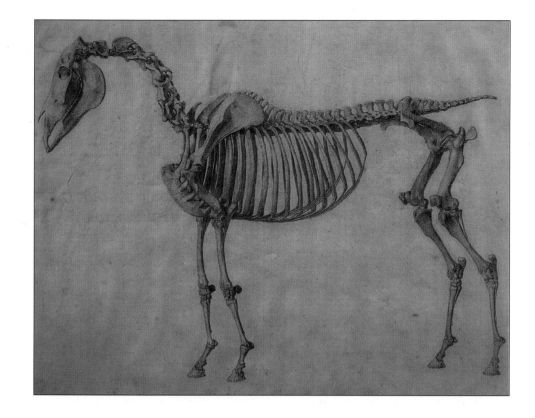

part of landscape or townscape. As
genre painting became commoner
from the Renaissance onwards, the
horse is also shown in stable and
farmyard. With the development of
the Thoroughbred and the fashion for
horseracing, the individual horse
portrait became common. It was often
commissioned by an owner as a record
of a cup-winner, although a farmer
might also sometimes commission a
travelling limner to make a picture of
a favourite riding or working horse.

As the role of the working horse
has faded, the plough horse and the
stage-coach team have gained an extra
romantic and nostalgic quality, but the
horse remains as much a subject for
the modern artist as for any in the
past. The contemporary painter and
sculptor often may not strive for the
exact visual likeness which the camera
now supplies, but the horse still
provides an inspiration for creating an
image that will capture its qualities.

The Origins of the Horse

The horse belongs to a family of animals that includes the zebra, onager and ass. Their ancestry can be traced to a Palaeocene animal type called Condylarthren, whose descendants also include the tapir and rhinoceros. One form of Condylarthren living in the Eocene period over 53 million years ago was *Hyracotherium,* more commonly called *Eohippus* (which means 'dawn horse'). Its fossilized bones have been found in vast numbers in what is now the southern United States. From there, when the land masses of Asia and America were still joined, it seems to have spread eastwards as far as Europe. *Eohippus* did not look much like a modern horse. It was only about 30 cm (12 inches) tall and had toes on its feet rather than hooves. It was more

like a fox-terrier dog or, as the people who gave it the name *Hyracotherium* thought, the little African and Asian animal called a hyrax or dassie.

Over the next 50 million years Eohippus evolved into the first fully hoofed horse, *Pliohippus*. About three times the size of its Palaeocene ancestor, *Pliohippus* looked like a horse and ate grass instead of leaves. By the time modern humans, *Homo sapiens*, appeared on the Earth 200,000 years ago *Pliohippus* had already evolved further into *Equus,* an animal over 120 cm (4 feet) high that was the foundation form of the modern horse. This too, appears to have originated in North America, spreading down into South America and westwards into Eurasia and Africa. All the other members of the equine family evolved from it. It is probable that the most primitive form spread across into Eurasia when the climate was still tropical; these became the asses and zebra of Africa. There were at least three broad types which can be recognized in the many kinds of domestic horse we know today, although almost all modern horse types were created deliberately by human control over breeding to develop horses with particular characteristics.

The Steppe type, which still survives in Przewalski's Horse, had a large head, short body, narrow hooves and a mane that stood up like a brush. The Forest type was heavier, with broader hooves adapted to marshy ground, a broad short head and a thick, hairy coat. It is now extinct, but its successors are the modern heavy horses. The third type was like the Tarpan, which may have been a direct survivor, although the last official Tarpan died in 1887 and the modern breed was founded from look-alikes from among Polish peasants' horses. It had a small, narrow head, a lightweight body and long, slim legs.

The original form of *Equus* became extinct about 8,000 years ago and all horses disappeared from the Americas until they were re-introduced by Europeans. Australia had separated from the other land masses before

Equus had evolved, and horses were taken there by settlers. The early horse types adapted further to different climates and conditions, and the modern breeds of horse and pony usually combine features of more than one type.

The earliest known depictions of the horse are cave paintings in France and Spain, which date back to 15,000 or even 20,000 years ago. We can only guess their purpose. Were they linked to some form of worship or were they part of some hunting magic? Perhaps both – but prehistoric cave paintings are often in places which are not easily accessible and it seems certain that they had some ritual purpose, rather than being created simply as decoration.

Early humans regarded the horse as an animal to be hunted for its flesh. When and where horses were first taken from the wild herds and brought under human control is not known. It was some time between 30,000 and 2,000 BC, long after dogs, sheep, llamas and cattle had become domestic animals. The first horse 'tamers' were probably among the nomadic peoples of the grasslands of the Eurasian steppes north of the Caucasus who had already become cattle herders and breeders.

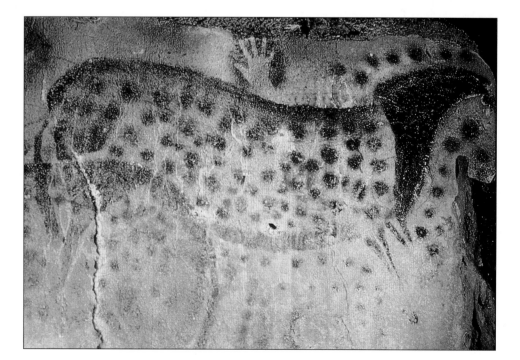

RIGHT
Train Landscape
by Eric Ravilious (1908-1942).
The huge white horse shown through the carriage window by this fine British illustrator, who died in World War II, is a familiar sight to rail travellers from London to the west of England. It was made in 1778 on a hillside to the west of Westbury in Wiltshire, by cutting away turf to reveal the chalk beneath. There was a vogue for making such figures in the eighteenth century, some as memorials to horses, but this one is believed to be on the site of an earlier figure.

BELOW
The horse in the Vale of the White Horse, near Uffington in Oxfordshire, probably dates from the Iron Age. It was made in the same way, by removing turf, but is much more stylized in form.

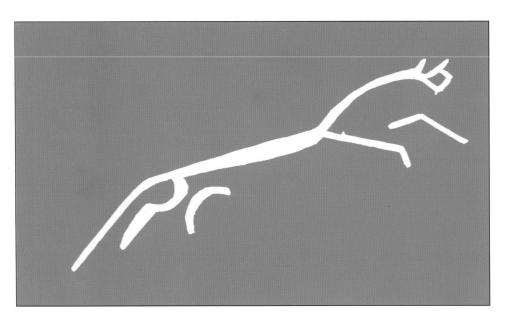

It is relatively easy to capture the young of wild cattle. Wild calves are left in cover while their mothers graze and, if discovered, they cower rather than run away. Foals, on the other hand, run with their mothers soon after birth and are more difficult to separate. Moreover, they run too fast for people to catch. Perhaps someone first captured an injured mare in foal or a new-born foal, still unsteady on its legs was captured by herdsmen and survived by suckling on a cow or goat.

When first domesticated, horses provided an additional, convenient source of food: mares were milked and fattened foal were eaten. To bring a mare into foal again, she was tethered where stallions from the wild herds could mate with her.

When were they first ridden or put into harness – and which came first? Sledges and ploughs with yokes for attachment to an animal have been found, dating back to 3,000 BC, but these were pulled by cattle. The first known wheel was made by a Sumerian craftsman in the fourth millennium BC, but oxen were the first haulage animals of Mesopotamia.

No doubt, the Eurasian nomads began by putting baggage across a horse's back and then, perhaps, placed a child on top of it. Next an adult may have tried to stay astride a sound animal, not an injured mare, as it bucked and reared like a bronco at a rodeo. Soon some foals would have been saved from the pot and reared to accept a human mount.

The travois was an early invention for haulage. Made of sticks tied in an A-shape with the open ends dragging on the ground and the load laid across it, it was pulled by both dogs and reindeer and probably used by the horse people. When knowledge of the wheel reached them, they adopted the cart and chariot and, in turn, horsemanship itself gradually spread to other peoples. The centaur of Greek mythology – half man, half horse – probably has its origins in confused reports of people riding which reached cultures that did not know the horse and so did not distinguish horse from rider. When native Americans first saw the mounted conquistadors they, too, are said to have thought them to be one creature.

riding was unknown. Similar misconceptions arose when the horseless people of Mexico first saw the mounted Spanish invaders. Although conquistador Hernan Cortes' cavalry consisted of only 16 horses, he attributed his victory over the Aztec forces to it.

The Horse
in the Ancient World

ABOVE
ABOVE
A wall painting from the tomb of the
sculptor Nebuman at Thebes (c. 1400 BC).
The upper chariot is drawn by a pair of
horses, the lower by either wild asses

(onagers) or mules. Both are harnessed in
a similar way, the shaft pulling the chariot
attached to a crosspiece between the two
horses. Despite their proximity to the
cornfield scene and the tree, these chariots

look unsuited to any agricultural purpose,
even carrying produce. Perhaps they were
used by overseers supervising the harvest.
It was the nomadic Hyksos from central
Asia who brought chariots to Egypt in the

12

As shown by this bas-relief and others from the royal palaces at Nineveh and Nimrud, the Assyrians had massive war chariots and also used chariots when the king went hunting. They had become riders, too, using saddle cloths. Assyrian art shows how riding positions changed from the seat of the ninth century BC, well back on the horse, almost on the croup, and gripping with the calves and heels, to the deep seat of the seventh century which enabled the rider to grip with the thighs. Assyrian armies were probably the first to use both chariots and mounted archers in battle.

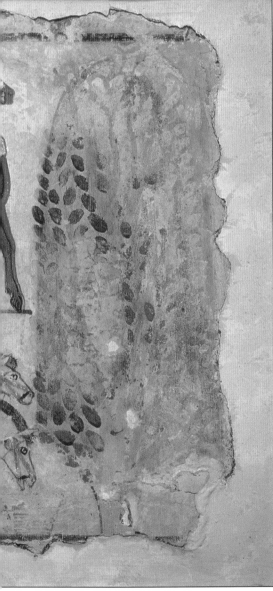

eighteenth century BC. They enabled these invaders to sweep through Syria and conquer the previously invincible Egyptian armies.

With the invention of the wheel, the Sumerians harnessed another species of the genus *Equus*, the wild ass or onager, to pull chariots, using them in pairs as they had used oxen for the plough. The Sumerian wheel was a solid disc, unable to turn independently. Indeed, turning was possible only with two-wheeled chariots and then at very slow speeds. The oldest form of cart, for which the earliest evidence has been found in Crete, had four wheels. This had little practical use and was probably used only for cult ceremonies. It was the invention of the spoked wheel mounted so that each wheel could turn independently on the axle which made turning at speed possible. Even then, it gave a very bumpy ride, although making the platform of a chariot from a bed of woven pliant material may have helped to reduce the jolting. It was not until the fifteenth century AD, when wheelwrights and carriage builders in the Hungarian town of Kocs developed a system of connecting the front and back axles of a four-wheel vehicle with a pole and suspending the carriage above this chassis on leather straps, that a more comfortable ride was possible.

Compared with the technology of later centuries the war chariot, drawn by asses as in the Chaldean army, or by horses, was a heavy and clumsy vehicle, useful only for a direct frontal attack on level ground. With faster horses and more manoeuvrability it could become a powerful weapon to drive into opposing infantry, especially when it was equipped with knives or scythes fitted to the wheels – a practice used by the Persian army of Darius in the east and -perhaps also used by Queen Bouddicca in Britain against the Romans.

For centuries Egyptian armies

secured the wealth of the Nile against invaders and extended Egyptian power until the eighteenth century BC, when they found they could not resist the invading Hyksos armies. These people from Asia, equipped with horse-drawn chariots, drove their conquering way through the countries of the eastern Mediterranean and took power in Egypt. From them the Egyptians learned to use horses and, in turn, rode out in their chariots to conquer. However, the days of the chariot for military use were numbered. Except in southern India, where they persisted as a weapon well into the fourth century of the modern era, they proved less effective than well-trained cavalry. Their use continued, however, in ceremonial parades, such as the triumphal processions of victorious Roman generals, and as a form of transport for officials travelling the length and breadth of the Empire along the well-paved Roman roads. Chariot-racing, too, remained a feature of the Roman games.

With the decline of the Roman Empire and the resultant poor maintenance of the Roman roads, wheeled transport became impracticable in much of Europe, especially in winter. It was easier to load goods onto a horse's back than to transport it in a cart that got stuck in mud or broke its wheels or axle on a rocky road. Carriages were little more than carts and provided no respite from the shakes and bumps as they trundled over uneven surfaces. While a litter slung between two horses might be used for the frail or elderly, most able-bodied people would find it faster and much more comfortable to ride – and if they could not afford a horse or donkey, they would walk.

RIGHT
Riders in the Panathenaic procession, part of the sculptured frieze of the Parthenon, the great temple of Athena on the Acropolis of Athens, designed by the sculptor Phidias. The young horsemen, who are riding bareback and well forward, may have been intended to represent the dead heroes of the battle of Marathon, for the temple was built in 447-438 BC to celebrate Athens' role in leading Greece to final victory against the Persians.

ABOVE RIGHT
A Roman mosaic from Carthage, dated about AD 500. Although the horse could, perhaps, be loosely identified as a Barb, the craftsmen making such mosaics often used standard motifs and did not work from life. By the end of the Imperial period, the Romans had a headstall and snaffle bridle, although they are not shown here. The Scythians had already developed a leather stirrup, but the Romans did not apparently have knowledge of it. Mounting without stirrups is not easy and Roman cavalry practised mounting and dismounting on wooden horses.

The Warhorse

There was a limit to the use of massed chariots, each with its charioteer and a fighting man – or two warriors in the case of the huge chariots seen in some Assyrian bas reliefs. Effective when used *en masse* on relatively smooth and level ground, they were easily halted by a ditch or an embankment. The forms of harness put enormous strain on horses going up a slope, and downhill there was a risk of the chariot's running onto the horse. Although it was to have an important role in communications and for hauling equipment and supplies when armies could not live off the land, it was as a mount that the horse gave the greatest military advantage.

The Persians and the Nubians were among the first to use cavalry. The ancient Greeks became proficient horsemen, too, but tended to use horses for reconnaissance rather than in battle, relying more on formations of foot-soldiers, the hoplites.

By the time of Alexander the Great horses played a greater military role. At the battle of Gaugamela in 331 BC the Greek forces consisted of 40,000 infantry and 7,000 horsemen – but they faced a Persian force of more than 134,000, of which 34,000 were cavalry with a front line of chariots.

The finest horsemen of this time were almost certainly the Scythians. They probably originated in central Asia, but by about 700 BC had reached Asia Minor and then came into conflict with Greece and Persia. They were a nomadic people, frequently on the move, although those in the west became more settled and developed outstanding skills as craftsmen. The Greek historian Herodotus describes

them as 'all equestrian archers'. While Greeks and Persians rode bareback or simply put a cloth on their horses to give a slightly firmer seat, the Scythians developed a much firmer saddle. This was a leather cushion stuffed with hair, slightly raised at the back and kept in position by a strap under the horse's belly. They may even have invented the stirrup, for there are signs that they may have used a leather loop on the saddle strap. A vase, discovered in a grave mound by the river Dneiper and dating from about 300 BC, shows a saddled horse with a rein that appears to end in a leather loop hanging on each side of the saddle. The stirrup as it is known today was probably invented by a people from the same steppe lands, the Huns. However, it was well over 1,000 years before it reached western Europe through contact with the Avars, yet another race of nomadic horse-archers. Meanwhile the Numidian horsemen (from what is now Algeria), who fought on both sides during the Punic Wars between Rome and Carthage a century later, were still riding bareback.

The Numidians carried small, round shields and a number of javelins which they used in hit-and-run attacks. For centuries western cavalry fought with spear and sword – Norman knights can be seen charging with spears held above their heads in the Bayeux tapestry, which records William the Conqueror's invasion of England. Although a spear could be thrown, their style of fighting required getting to comparatively close quarters. Under a hail of arrows from

mounted archers a shield and body armour became essential. More effective armour for both rider and mount meant greater weight. Huge horses that could carry much heavier weights were bred.

These great warhorses were also weapons in themselves. Their front feet were shod with projecting stud-like nails the more effectively to trample the enemy. In a charge, their stability and greater weight also increased the thrust behind the lance with which the medieval knight became equipped. The lance was carried low, not held overhead.

With the development of effective firearms, heavy armour became obsolete. Pistols could be much more readily fired from the saddle than the crossbows and longbows of European and English armies. The French, at the battle of Cerisoles in 1544, appear to have been the first to introduce the new tactic of a squadron of cavalry riding up to a square of foot soldiers, each rank cantering off to the side as they reached the front and discharging their shots, then wheeling back to the rear of the column to reload before advancing to fire again.

Cavalry now developed into three groups: dragoons, mounted on heavy, cob-type horses, who were virtually infantry on horseback; lancers (or cuirassiers), who rode the best big horses for heavy charges; and hussars, on the best light horses, used for sudden attacks and forays. A massed cavalry charge could sometimes overwhelm by the sheer weight of men and horses, especially if used immediately after an artillery bombardment had confused and

A Mongol Archer on Horseback, a Chinese ink and colour drawing dating from the Ming Dynasty (1368-1644). The owners' seals include that of the Emperor Ch'ien Lung. The horse is one of the sturdy Steppe ponies, without the middle eastern ancestry seen in the Chinese horses on page 39. Marco Polo described the Mongols' horses as 'so well broken to quick changes of movement that upon the signal given, they instantly turn in every direction, and by these rapid manoeuvres many victories have been obtained'. He describes how the Mongol armies never mixed with the enemy, but hovered about, discharging arrows first from one side and then the other. They sometimes pretended flight, shooting back at their pursuers, who thought they were winning when, in fact, they were losing a battle, for the Mongols would then wheel about and overpower them. However, as Yeh-lu T'su T'ai, a Chinese general who switched to support the Mongols, said 'The Empire was won on horseback, but you cannot govern from the saddle'.

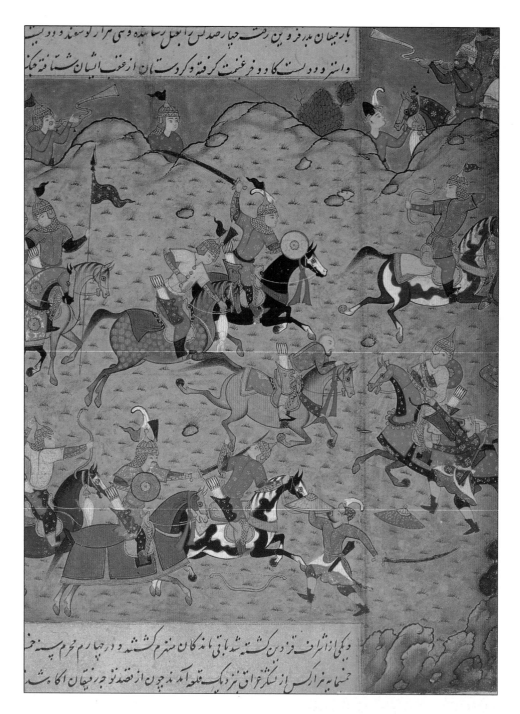

LEFT
A page from the Iskender Namah,
*a fifteenth-century Persian manuscript of
the poet Nizami's retelling of the life of
Alexander the Great 1,800 years before,
but showing contemporary warfare. The
soldiers are all equipped with both swords
and bows and arrows. The foreground
horse and two of the others are wearing
protective armour on the head and body.*

RIGHT
Horses Crossing a River
*by Zhao Mengfu (1254-1322). By the
most famous artist of the Mongol period,
this picture was painted at the time of
Kublai Khan, when Marco Polo made his
travels through the Mongol lands and
China. The conquering Mongol armies of
Genghis Khan consisted entirely of
horsemen. Their mounts provided milk,
which was made into cheese or fermented
to produce an alcoholic drink called
kumiss. Horse flesh was also dried and
Polo tells how, on campaign, riders would
also open up a vein and drink the horse's
blood for sustenance. Kublai Khan
transferred his capital to Beijing (Peking)
and adopted many of the refinements of
Chinese life. These horses are not typical
Mongol mounts, but reflect the
introduction of middle eastern stock to
China 1,000 years earlier. Various owners
have marked the picture with their red seal
impressions.*

terrified the enemy. This was a tactic which Napoleon was to use towards the end of his career, although it failed him at Waterloo because there was too steep a gradient on the heavy ground and his horses were in poor condition.

The pointlessness of riding straight into the cannon's mouth was demonstrated in the famous 'Charge of the Light Brigade' in the Crimean War in 1854. As the result of a mistaken order, 673 horses charged the Russian guns; only 260 survived. As a

French general exclaimed, 'C'est magnifique, mais ce n'est pas la guerre' (it is magnificent, but it is not war).

During the American Civil War there were some heroic mounted raids by both Northern and Southern forces, and the U.S. cavalry had a prominent role in the exploitation of the American West – facing Native Americans who, although horses had been part of their culture for only two centuries, had developed a horsemanship comparable to that of

the peoples of the Asian steppes. However, the cavalry charge was not to survive against shrapnel and automatic weapons.

Horses still played an important part in warfare right up to World War I (1914-18). Millions of horses were involved; it has been estimated that more saddle horses were deployed than in any previous war. Family mounts, children's ponies and commercial horses were conscripted for army use. On the Eastern Front,

A Chinese pottery figure of a horse in the style of the Tang period (618-906). Such horse figures were often used as offerings in the graves of the Imperial family. The saddle has a raised front and rear edge and there is a metal ring stirrup hanging in a forward position over the saddlecloth. The Chinese adopted the stirrup from the Huns. Chinese horses were mainly Mongol ponies until the Han period (206 BC-AD 221), when expeditions to Persia brought back Persian stallions for breeding.

German, Austrian and Russian armies put many cavalry divisions in the field. Large cavalry forces were also assembled in the west, but the pattern of warfare on that front did not provide the opportunities for them to be used. Horses were essential as draught animals, bringing up supplies and hauling artillery into position – and it took as many as a dozen horses to pull some of the heavier cannon.

Long-range, heavy artillery and automatic weapons made the cavalry charge a thing of the past, although in September 1939 the Polish army, in an heroic but hopeless attempt to stem the advance of invading German tanks, launched its crack mounted division against them. Nevertheless, horses still had a role in World War II. The German army used some 2.75 million horses, over 50,000 of which were killed in the Battle of Stalingrad. The Red Army had over 3.5 million horses. Their tanks were usually accompanied by mounted units. Cossack units were used for reconnaissance, especially in winter, and for rounding up German stragglers. Japanese forces also used cavalry in the same way in their conquest of China and Manchuria.

An illumination from a mid-sixteenth-century account of the triumphs of the Emperor Charles V, painted in Rome. The Emperor is shown raising the siege of Vienna in 1529. His horse's head and neck are closely encased in plate armour. Padded covers give the body some protection and one of the horses on the right has plate armour panels over a quilted cover. Carvings on Trajan's Column show Roman cavalry facing Asiatic horsemen whose mounts are clad in a scale-like, close-fitting armour over their entire bodies, heads and legs. Although small plates sewn to cloth were used as body armour from early times, it would be impossible to fit this closely all over a horse. Quilted leather was the usual protection worn by Asian horses. In medieval Europe, by the later part of the fifteenth century, the horse's head armour might consist of hinged plates over the front of the face and covering the mane, with chain mail hanging down over the neck. The flanks were protected by a shell-like panel on either side and there was a frontal 'skirt' of hinged plates across the chest. The heavier the armour of both horse and rider became, the more massive the horse had to be, with a consequent loss of manoeuvrability.

RVNT:ADMON TE MICHAELIS ET

The Polish Rider
by Rembrandt Harmensz van Rijn (1606-69).
Art historians have recently decided that this picture is probably not by the great Dutch master, but it is still a fine painting. It was painted about 1650. It is not known whether this is a portrait or a general image of a knight on horseback and there is no real evidence for the identification 'Polish', although the hat and quiver suggest eastern rather than western Europe. Fast and manoeuvrable, with cutting weapons on both sides and an axe as well as bow and arrows, he is more like the Mongol horseman than the heavy medieval knight.

LEFT

The eleventh-century embroidery usually known as the Bayeaux Tapestry provides, in picture-strip, the Norman version of how William I (the 'Conqueror') claimed and gained the English crown. In this scene, Earl Harold of Wessex is seen with William of Normandy passing Mont St. Michel while on a military expedition against Count Conan of Brittany. William, wearing a quilted tunic and carrying a mace, and Harold, in front of him, do not appear to be wearing armour, although the knight behind has a helmet and full suit of mail. The rider in front of them is not riding side-saddle, but probably dismounting because the next images show that there are quicksands in the river they have to cross. The tapestry shows quite clearly that the stirrup has now reached western Europe. However, Harold's Saxons fought on foot, and their defeat when William invaded England was mainly due to the power of the Norman cavalry.

LEFT

Red Indian Horsemanship
by George Catlin (1794-1872).
A self-taught American painter fascinated by Native American life, Catlin painted many such subjects which, in his own time, were better received in Europe than in the United States. The introduction of the horse brought many changes to the culture of the peoples of the plains, not only in hunting but in resisting the advance of the white intruders. The Navaho and the Apache, followed by the Pawnee and Comanche soon became excellent horsemen, and they achieved their skills without the use of stirrups.

The Charge of the Scots Greys at Waterloo
by Elizabeth Butler (1846-1933). A popular British artist for her mainly military scenes, she painted this 66 years after the famous battle of 1815. It is also known as **Scotland Forever.** *It gives a stirring impression of what a cavalry charge was like, and its appeal to patriotic sentiment is characteristic of her work.*

ABOVE
Travoys Arriving with Wounded at a Dressing Station, Smol, Macedonia, 1919
by Stanley Spencer (1891-1959).
In the Medical Corps, and for all kinds of transport, horses were still vital in World War I. There were huge losses of horse as well as human lives. The British army fielded a strong veterinary service and saved some three-quarters of the more than 2.5 million horses and mules they treated during the four-year conflict.

BELOW
Guernica
by Pablo Picasso (1881-1973). The Spanish artist's huge painting was his response to the German bombing of the Basque town of Guernica in 1937 during the Spanish Civil War. The horse is, perhaps, even more expressive than the human victims of the anguish of the innocent and the horror of the anti-fascist world at this event which presaged so many similar terrors in the years that have followed.

this could have been left out — happily

The Working Horse

The horse has been exploited in all manner of ways. It has provided milk, meat and hide. It has carried loads, pulled the plough and cart, the wagon train and the stagecoach. It has borne all kinds on its back: the soldier and the courier, the merchant and the parson, the doctor and the highwayman. It has turned the mill wheel and the treadmill and, when worn out by labour, been consigned to the knacker's yard for its bones to be boiled up for glue. At the beginning of the twentieth century, one London knacker alone was killing 26,000 horses every year, at an average age of about 11 years.

The economic importance of the horse was inestimable. It was vital to transport and industry – we still sometimes rate the output of machines by their horsepower! The sight of a great Shire horse gives an immediate impression of its strength and power, but horses have been specially bred to produce this kind of strength. It was the ox that originally pulled the wagon and drew the plough; the early horse was not strong enough. Nor was it tractable: a listing in a Hittite legal code gives a chariot horse a higher value than a plough-ox, but rates a mule (the cross between a horse and a donkey) at three times higher, probably because of its greater adaptability.

It was as a pack-carrying animal that the horse was first put to work. A train of pack animals was the backbone of transport in the Roman Empire and remained so in Europe throughout the Middle Ages. Together with donkeys and mules, the horse still plays this useful role in rocky, steep country that lacks good roads, in places where the terrain makes wheeled transport impracticable and on land where a vehicle would get stuck in deep, heavy mud.

One north British breed, the Chapman Horse, got its name from the chapmen, or merchants, of medieval times. Although it no longer carries the products of the cloth-trade across the Pennines or on the roads to London, the ancient breed survives, with the addition of some Thoroughbred blood, in what is now known as the Cleveland Bay – a carriage horse in the breeding of which Queen Elizabeth II has shown particular interest.

Some idea of the economic importance of the packhorse is demonstrated by the regular service of pack-trains which operated to a strict timetable between London and Exeter, county town of Devonshire about 290 km (180 miles) of the English capital. Pack-teams were the carriers for the English cloth trade for another hundred years, but the building of

An illumination from the Luttrell Psalter, commissioned by Sir Geoffrey Luttrell of Irnham, Lincolnshire about 1340. Its illustrations include many scenes of country life. Here a team of horses, with one in the shafts and two in the traces, is having a hard time pulling a heavy cart uphill, and three peasants have to push at the rear. Both the iron-bound wheel rims and the horses' hooves have metal studs to help their grip on poor roads and tracks.

RIGHT
A late seventeenth-century print of clothmakers in the north of England transporting their wares along one of the packhorse trails. The horse was probably used as a pack animal long before anyone rode its back or used it to pull a cart.

BELOW
The Harrowing Team
by John Frederick Herring, Senior (1795-1865).
The harrow breaks up clumps of earth and prepares the ground for cultivation after ploughing.

turnpike roads, canals and then the railways reduced the need for packhorses on long-distance routes, and by the middle of the eighteenth century their commercial role in Britain was already much reduced. As other forms of transport became more efficient, the packhorse was used only by small-scale traders and peddlers and for carrying goods in remote areas.

Carts during the Middle Ages tended to be either square-shaped tumbrels of solid planks or lighter boxes of latticed willow. Some medieval illustrations show studded wheel-rims which helped the grip on difficult terrain. Nevertheless, a heavy load required much greater pulling power than would be needed on a good modern surface, so teams of horses were harnessed to pull together. Efficiency was helped by the invention of a proper horse-collar; the rigid padded form used today is unchanged in type from those depicted by artists in the fourteenth century.

It was probably quicker – and certainly more comfortable – to walk rather than ride in one of these carts. Those few members of the nobility who owned carriages did little better. A carriage would be covered by an arched canopy to keep out the wind, rain or scorching sun, was probably hung with tapestries or embroideries and might have carved and gilded wheels, but the only protection from the bumps and jolts would be a pile of

cushions. Such carriages cost a fortune. The sister of King Edward III of England owned one that cost £1,000 – enough to buy 2,000 cows or 240,000 chickens at fourteenth-century prices.

Carriages were useful in towns where roads were surfaced and for travelling short distances. They were also used for pageants and processions where show was more important than transportation.

Travelling in a horse litter was somewhat more comfortable. This was similar to the litter carried by servants, but borne on shafts between two horses, one in front and one behind. It might give emphasis to rank and gentility, but only those who were not able to ride would be likely to prefer it.

ABOVE
The Drinking Place
by Stanhope Alexander Forbes
(1857-1947).
The artist was a leading member of the Newlyn School of painters working in that Cornish fishing village. They were leaders in British plein air *(outdoor), as opposed to studio, painting in the last decades of the nineteenth century.*

A vehicle called a whirlicote was known as early as the reign of King Richard II of England. It consisted of a hammock slung on the standards of a wagon and used for carrying royal or noble ladies who were too fragile to ride a horse, but no more seems to have been heard of it. It was probably expensive and made travelling rather like being on a stormy sea.

Coach suspension on leather straps, which had developed in Hungary, did begin to reach western Europe in the sixteenth century, but, as late as 1639, the 'coch' of the wealthy Verney family of Buckinghamshire could still be described as 'a sort of cart without springs, with leathern curtains against the weather, which most unluxurious luxury was used only by infirm persons or delicate women who could not ride'. Nevertheless, roads and vehicles were improving, and in 1625 a patent was granted for a method of using metal springs to support the passenger compartment – although it was many decades before this was used effectively.

When the development of effective musketry and cannon made the armour-carrying great horses of the military redundant, these powerful animals became available to replace plough-oxen and haul wagons. This change was very noticeable in England in the seventeenth century. During the Civil War between King Charles I and Parliament, large numbers of heavy horses had been bred and imported for the armies on both sides. While the nobleman's horse, often with Andalusian blood, would continue as a riding horse, the heavier animals were too slow; in the shafts, however, they had great pulling power.

Nevertheless, coaches were increasingly common. A character in Middleton and Dekker's play *The Roaring Girl* (1611) complains about the way they block the streets in London. In the same period, Thames watermen, who made their living rowing passengers up and down river and across the Thames, complained that coaches were taking away their living. In the mid-seventeenth century

ABOVE

The Last Furrow

by Henry Hubert La Thangue (1859-1929). Although most heavy working horses owe their origins to the old warhorses of Europe, the modern working breeds were not established until comparatively recently. The Suffolk Punch is mentioned as early as 1506, but all modern examples go back to a

single chestnut trotting horse foaled in 1760. The Clydesdale was also a mid-eighteenth century development in the coalfields of Lanarkshire. Along with the Shire, Percheron, Ardennais and other 'improved' heavy breeds, they developed at a time when new machinery was being introduced on farms. They were used for pulling this as well as heavy wagons.

there were regular public coach services from London to cities as far away as Exeter (taking four days) and Durham (no time specified). Shopkeepers a century later were still complaining about the way the streets were blocked by 'Hackney' carriages standing for hire – London seems always to have had a traffic problem!

Hackney (often shortened to hack), a term for a hired horse since the fourteenth century, may be derived from the name of the district, then just beyond London's city walls, because this was where horses were raised, or, perhaps, because it was the first village near London that provided carriages for occasional passengers. There is another possible derivation of the word: the old Norman French *haquenai*, was applied to riding animals of the humblest type. It crops up, used rudely of a horse, by the poet Chaucer, as 'Hakenay'

Londoners also complained about the deep ruts in their roads which 'tossed and jumbled' their coaches so much 'that it has been near an hour e'er they could recover the use of their limbs'. As for country roads – when

BELOW
The Slate Quarry
a painting of c. 1778-95 by an unknown artist, but someone closely influenced by George Stubbs. The carters are having some trouble getting these horses started with their heavy load.

the Emperor Charles VI on a visit to England in 1703 decided to travel the 80 km (50 miles) from London to Petworth by coach, it took three days. The coach was overturned a dozen times and the journey was completed only by hiring a gang of Sussex labourers to hold it upright and put their shoulders to the wheels to get it through the mud. Nonetheless, the eighteenth century saw a considerable improvement in highway standards through legislation and Turnpike Trusts, and Britain soon had a service of stagecoaches and mail carriers that was the envy of other nations. New road building methods introduced by the Scottish engineers Thomas Telford and John McAdam made smoother and faster running possible. This, in turn, produced a

demand for a superior type of horse that could deliver a competitive service.

The development of canals in the later part of the seventeenth century transferred some freight from road to water, but also gave more work to horses. Convenience and economy, rather than speed, were the great advantages of the waterways; the strong, slow, heavy horse was ideal for canal work, hauling barges. They were useful, too, for hauling the agricultural machinery which began to appear at this time.

The first railways, which were in mines and mining areas, relied on pit ponies and horses. As the development of steam locomotives and the rapid replacement of the stagecoach by rail travel reduced one demand for horses, another developed. Increased passenger travel and burgeoning manufacturing industry required an expanding number of carts, carriages and horses to and from the stations and the goods' yards. In cities, local omnibus and tramway systems called for yet more horses.

In North America and in other countries where the railway networks were not so highly developed, horse transport continued to be the major form of transportation, even over long distances. However, by the beginning of the twentieth century a new form of locomotion was attracting attention – the petrol-driven horseless carriage. Within a decade or so, the motor car and motor bus had made horse-drawn passenger transport the exception in most of the western world. For goods' haulage, door-to-door deliveries and on the farm, the horse was still a familiar sight until after World War II, but then became a rarity.

LEFT
A miniature from the Luttrell Psalter.
In 1340 it took five horses to haul this heavy wagon, which must then have been considered the height of royal luxury for passengers.

LEFT
The Barge Horses
by Jules Veyrassat (1828-93).
The type is like that of the Boulonnais, a breed developed in northern France. These horses appear to be pulling a sailing barge against the current on a Continental river. The spread of canal systems over England in the eighteenth and early nineteenth centuries enabled a draught horse to pull weights as heavy as six times those which it could haul in a wagon on the roadways.

ABOVE
The Reverend Carter Thelwell and Family
by George Stubbs (1724-1806). The country parson with his church, his riding horse and his wife and child in their pony cart.

OVERLEAF
Barnet Fair
by John Frederick Herring, Senior (1795-1865). This famous horse fair held at Barnet Village, north of London and now part of metropolitan Greater London, continued until the middle of the twentieth century. The common is traversed by the Great North Road and, behind the gentleman being driven in his trap, a stagecoach is approaching between the groups of horses brought for sale. It was part of a regular service carrying passengers and the Royal Mail from Glasgow in Scotland all the way to London. The journey south took two and a half days. Each stage was strictly timed, as were stops for meals and to do post office business. Horses were ready waiting and four minutes were allowed to get them changed and off again.

The Riding Horse

The early forms of horse were probably too small to carry a man on their backs, even if people had tried to make them do so. Smaller ponies may be suitable only for children and the smallest breed of horse, the Falabella, standing at only seven hands high, 72 cm (28 inches) at the withers, is too small to be a saddle horse even for a child. Almost every other kind of horse probably has been or is ridden at some time or another. Some breeds have been created for specific tasks – to add power to a cavalry charge or haul a heavy dray and, in recent times, with an eye on their use for sporting purposes – but through the centuries it is used as a mount suited to a particular type of rider that has differentiated most horses.

The Steppe horses used by the Celts and the Germanic tribes tended to be small, but fast and agile. Although in Europe the heavier, slower type, known as the cold-blooded horses, provided the medieval warhorse and, later, haulage horses, there was a practical demand for much more versatile mounts. (Cold-blooded horses were so-called from the German *Kaltblutigkeit,* which refers to their cool, phlegmatic temperament and has nothing to do with their circulation.) Even the military needed sumpter horses, or packhorses, to carry baggage and equipment, a fast horse or courser for communications, a less ponderous horse for a knight to ride when not in action, then known as a Palfrey, and a Rouncey, an all-purpose horse to serve the squire who rode behind the knight he served.

The Palfrey had a very even gait. Both legs on each side came forward together in the pace; changing to a faster speed, the rack, they moved independently in succession. In both gaits the horse could accelerate smoothly from an amble to a gallop. Such a comfortable horse became the travelling horse of the more affluent. The Rouncey, a trotting horse, and the Hackney were general-purpose animals. (Hack was later used to mean a horse ridden to the meet before the rider transferred to a hunter. Today, it

can mean a variety of different riding horses, according to local usage, and need have no pejorative meaning.)

Every country has developed its own horses or ponies which have provided local mounts, but most now show the influence of types from very distant lands. Most noticeable in the riding horse has been the introduction of horses originally bred in the Islamic world.

The wild horses of the mountains of northwest Africa were comparatively large but lightly built animals. The smaller horses of the deserts of Arabia and southwest Asia were also light-boned and graceful. A

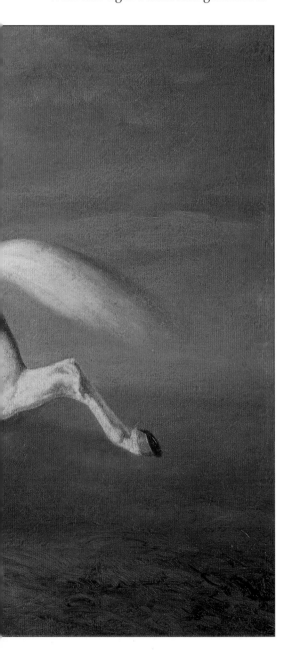

BELOW LEFT
The Pasha's Pride
by Alfred de Dreux (1810-60).
Its desert background has given the Arab the best stamina of any horse. Although small compared with many European breeds, it can carry a full-grown man with ease. When Napoleon's army was forced to retreat from Moscow in the bitter Russian winter of 1812 the Emperor's aide-de-camp recorded: 'The Arab horse withstood the exertions and privations better than the European horse; almost all the horses the Emperor had left were his Arabs.'

ABOVE
A Moghul painting of the early seventeenth-century of Shah Jehan and his wife. Below, the horse has a high saddle.

BELOW
The Good Samaritan
an etching by Rembrandt Harmensz van Rijn (1606-69).
This short-legged, sturdy horse is a Palfrey, the favoured riding horse of those who could afford it from the Middle Ages through to the seventeenth century.

poetic Moslem tradition says that the fleet Arab horse was created by Allah Himself from a handful of the south wind. A legend tells how the Prophet Mohammed ordered a herd of horses to be left for seven days without water. When they were released they raced to their watering place, but the Prophet then sounded the call to battle and immediately five mares came directly to him without stopping to drink. All pure-bred Arab horses are said to be descended from these mares.

The Quran instructs all believers to care well for their horses. In return, these horses offer prodigious courage and stamina. As Islam moved across north Africa, Arab blood was added to the African horse and the foundation type we know as the Barb went with the Islamic conquerors across the Straits of Gibraltar. There it produced the Andalusian. The influence of the Barb through the Andalusian and of Arab blood through contacts in the Crusades and later, was to lead to a whole range of lighter riding and racing horses.

By 1066 William the Conqueror was already riding an Andalusian, although no one else in his invading army did, as such horses were very expensive. From the Andalusian came the Alter Real of Portugal, the (now extinct) Neapolitan, the Aldruber and the Lipizanners of Vienna's Spanish Riding School.

Many American horse breeds stem from the Andalusian. Mustangs, for instance, are descended from horses brought over by Spanish settlers. Some of these became feral and roamed wild for 300 years, developing hardiness and independence, before they were redomesticated, although they now *not all thankfully* show the addition of other blood. The agile Criollo of Argentina is another direct descendant of the Andalusian, which has adapted to the conditions of the pampas. So too, are the Peruvian Stepping Horse and the Paso Fino of Puerto Rico. The American Quarterhorse, developed in Virginia and the Carolinas, is another with Arab, Barb and Andalusian blood. It was crossed with horses that arrived from England in early colonial days to produce a horse that earned its name from its prowess in sprint races over a quarter-mile distance.

The Arab horse played a major part in the development of the English Thoroughbred, created by racing enthusiasts in the seventeenth and early eighteenth centuries. Then, towards the end of the eighteenth

A Chinese painting dating from the seventeenth century showing the much earlier Emperor Yang (605-18) riding in his garden with his concubines. The artist has attributed to them all sufficient riding skill to control their mounts at the same time as they are playing their instruments – which include a kind of harp.

century, Arab blood was used to refine the old medieval Norman warhorse and, through further crosses with Thoroughbreds and other English horses, the Anglo Norman and the recent Selle Français – established only in 1958 – were produced.

The creation of new breeds and the improvement of old ones is a continuing process. Another recent riding horse is the Budyonny, named for the Russian revolutionary cavalry leader who instigated its creation in the Red Army stud at Rostov. It began

with a Thoroughbred-Don cross, with additions of Kazakh pony and Kirgiz blood. The ancient Kirgiz has been revitalized to produce the new Kirgiz.

People in continental European seem more concerned with owning a specific breed than those in the

performance. In the English-speaking countries a number of broad types have developed in response to particular demands for horses or ponies, without trying to establish any strain as a distinctive breed. Most will have a Thoroughbred or an Arab in their parentage. They can be roughly divided into the Cob, the Hack, the Hunter (or Jumper as it is called in the United States if it is used only for

BELOW
White Stallion by James Ward (1769-1859). A painter of genre scenes of country life (like those of his brother-in-law George Morland), from his thirties Ward began to concentrate on animals in landscape settings. His works were usually more dramatic and romantic than the equestrian portraits of Stubbs and Agasse.

English-speaking world. While continental breeders pay great attention to a well-curved neck, well-shaped rump and the high knee action capable of doing the Spanish walk, Britons, Americans and Australians are more concerned with a horse's

show jumping in an arena), the Riding Pony and the Polo Pony.

The Cob is small, compact and muscular – the modern equivalent of the medieval Rouncey. The Hack can be any of a wide range of horses ridden for pleasure, while Hunters and Polo pony are self-explanatory names.

It is an interesting footnote that, although a Celtic carving from a temple at Altbach shows a goddess sitting sideways on a horse, it was usual for both men and women to ride astride. In England it was not common for women to ride side-saddle until the fourteenth century. One of the earliest illustrations to show a woman doing so is in a manuscript copy of the Canterbury Tales, in which the Prioress is shown riding the new way, while the Wife of Bath is clearly sitting astride.

LEFT
Snake Indians
by Alfred Jacob Miller (1810-74). The Mustang of the American West was not an indigenous type, but a feral horse descended from the mounts brought to Mexico by Spanish conquistadors. It eventually reached the plains thousands of miles to the north, but in the wild it developed a lighter frame. To this stock was added that of horses frightened away from U.S. Cavalry camps and others lost by Europeans. Artist George Catlin described them as 'small, but very powerful with an exceedingly prominent eye, sharp nose, high nostril, small feet and delicate leg'. These and horses they captured from Europeans formed the mounts of the Native Americans.

LEFT
Mlle Croizette,
1873 by Charles Emile Auguste Carolus-Duran. The French both for riding side-saddle and the lady's costume was, rather inappropriately, Amazones. By the mid-nineteenth century, this was considered the only way for a fine lady to ride (lower-class tradeswomen were more likely to go in a gig or trap). This was mainly because sitting astride was considered indelicate.

BELOW LEFT
Horses and Dogs
by John Emms (1843-1912).
A horse expresses friendship and reassurance by laying its head across another horse's neck, often making a whickering sound. Friends greet by breathing into each other's nostrils often approaching frontally and offer mutual grooming, nibbling at each other's necks, pulling loose hair and skin from the mane, then moving down the body to the tail.

BELOW
The Arab Tent
by Sir Edwin Landseer (1802-73).
A new-born foal may be struggling unsteadily to its feet within minutes of being born and should be standing at least within the hour. It needs to be up and running as soon as possible to have any chance of survival against predators in the wild. The mare will usually keep other horses away at first, giving the foal a chance to become familiar with her appearance and smell. Later, if it strays, she will warn of danger and recall it with a high-pitched whinnying. The foal, if frightened, will call her with a shrill cry to which she responds with a deep rumbling call. Under natural conditions she will suckle the foal for almost a year – and longer if she does not become pregnant again – although at most studs, foals are forcibly weaned at six months old.

Horses at Skirling Fair
by James Howe (1780-1836).
Horses, ponies, traders and horsemen of every sort gather at a country fair. In many places, these horse fairs were – and some still are – regular events.

45

LEFT
Branding a Steer
by Frederic Remington (1861-1909)
the American painter famous for his
portrayal of the 'Wild West'. Without the
horse the opening up of the American
West and the cowboy's work with cattle
would have been impossible, especially on
the vast scale of ranching which was
developed.

ABOVE
Arab Huntsman Chased by Lions
by William Strutt (1825-1915).
Faced by danger, a horse's instinctive reaction is to flee as fast as possible. Horses at speed lay back their ears to keep dust and insects from being caught in their apertures, but the laid-back ear is also a sign of aggression and fear. Flaring nostrils and a curled-back lip, together with short, snorting breaths, are other signs of nervousness and fear, which will also produce sweating on the neck, behind the ears and between the hind legs.

LEFT
A Grey Arab Stallion in a Wooded Landscape
by Jaques-Laurent Agasse (1767-1844). This Swiss-born animal painter studied veterinary science in Paris at the same time as he was at David's school. He took up residence in England in 1800 and there, much influenced by the work of Stubbs, became his chief successor.

BELOW LEFT
Two Horses in a Wooded Landscape
by George Stubbs (1724-1806). A dark bay and a grey by the great English horse artist.

BELOW
The Morning Ride
by Sir Alfred Munnings (1878-1959). This English painter, President of the Royal Academy 1944-9, was an opponent of modern trends in art and was himself denigrated for his old-fashioned and somewhat slick style. However, he had a deep interest in horses and often painted them superbly.

By the mid-twentieth century side-saddle was no longer de rigeur for women, although Queen Elizabeth II used to ride in this way at the annual Trooping the Colour ceremony. Before the Middle Ages both men and women rode astride as most do today. However a century ago, in 1890 James Fillis argued in his **Breaking and Riding:** 'The great want in a man's seat is firmness, which would be still more difficult for a woman to acquire if she rode in a cross-saddle, because her thighs are rounder and weaker than those of a man. Discussion of this subject is, therefore, useless. Ladies who ride astride get such bad falls that they soon give up this practice.'

Haute École & Showmanship

Who can fail to admire fine horsemanship? The development of skill, rapport and control in horse and rider makes them more effective in warfare, sport or communications and adds great pleasure to the act of riding. The display of that control in ritual, competition and entertainment has a long history.

In Homer's *Iliad*, there is a description of horsemen circling the funeral pyre of Patroclus. The 'Trojan Game' is one name for figure riding, for it was believed to have originated in Troy as an equestrian sport for boy riders who made intricate manoeuvres, splitting into groups to circle, about turn and make formations. All this was good training for future cavalry. Ascanius, son of Aeneas, was said to have taken the Trojan Game to Italy.

The first known writer on the art of horsemanship was an Athenian called Simon in about 400 BC. We know him only through the general and historian Xenophon (c. 431-355 BC) whose *Peri hippikes* ('On Horsemanship') and *Hipparchikos* ('The Art of Horsemanship') cover the care, training and psychology of the horse, as well as riding.

Xenophon had been a mercenary with the Persians and he may have learned things from them which were new to his Greek contemporaries. His book was intended for riders whose horses were small, who lacked stirrups, rode bareback or only with a saddle cloth and had only a simple snaffle rather than a modern bit. His advice and exercises are not always appropriate for later riders, but it was his manual that led to the development of modern dressage.

Stylish equestrian display was probably common to all horse peoples. A report by the Byzantine historian Procopius of Belisarius' defeat of the Gothic King Totila in AD 552 describes how, in a ploy to delay battle while awaiting reinforcements, Totila, in shining gold armour, rode his large horse out into the space between the armies to perform the 'dance under arms': 'He wheeled his horse round in a circle and then turned him again to the other side and so made him run round and round. As he rode, he hurled his javelin into the air and caught it again as it quivered above him, then passed it rapidly from hand to hand, with great skill. He gloried in his ability in these things, falling back on his shoulders, spreading his legs and leaning from side to side, like a person who has from childhood precisely been taught the art of dancing.'

Xenophon's books on the horse were rediscovered in the Renaissance and were carefully studied by Federico Grisone, a Neapolitan nobleman. In 1532 he opened a riding academy which soon attracted pupils from the courts of Europe. In 1550 he published his own book *Gli Ordini di Cavalcare* ('The Rules of Horsemanship'), which lifted considerable material direct from Xenophon, although the use of brute-force methods of teaching are not found in the Greek!

Through his pupils the influence of the school spread. In France, Antoine de Pluvinel, sometime Master of the Duke of Anjou's riding stables, founded an Academy in Paris in 1594. His most famous pupil was the young King Louis XIII and the royal connection was exploited in his book *L'Instruction du Roi,* published after his

death in 1622 as *La Manège Royale* ('The Royal Riding School') – *manège* means both the exercises and the place where they are done – with many fine engravings by Crispin de Passe.

In Germany Georg von Löhneysen, an equerry at the princely stables at Wolfenbütell, became the leading instructor and author, while the most important English teacher was William Cavendish, Duke of Newcastle. Cavendish, in self-imposed exile since his defeat in the English Civil War, founded a riding school in Antwerp in premises behind Ruben's old house which were rented from the painter's widow. Cavendish's book, *A General System of Horsemanship in All Its Branches* was written and first published in French. It, too, is illustrated with fine engravings.

The methods and traditions established by these authors, teachers and horsemen were continued by others, such as François Robichon de la Guerinière in the following century and François Baucher in the nineteenth. They can still be seen in the Spanish Riding School in Vienna ('Spanish' because the famous Lipizzaner Greys originally came from Spain) and at the French Cavalry School at Saumur.

Equestrian *haute école* no longer has any practical military application, although mounted regiments play a significant part in ceremonials. Dressage, however, is still important to the serious rider and is a major competitive event at shows or when performed as a 'musical ride'.

Acrobatics performed on horseback were part of the Olympic Games in 1928, and in recent decades have become a popular competition at both national and international level.

LEFT
Traverse Between the Pillars
engraving by Crispin de Passe from
Antoine de Pluvinel's **L'Instruction du
Roi.** *The traverse is a movement on two
tracks: with the head facing the front, the
forelegs move along one line and the
hindlegs along a parallel one. Pluvinel, his
hat in his hand, is shown explaining to
the young king who is on the far right.
He often worked with horses tied between
two 2-metre (7-foot) high pillars, a method
copied by other schools.*

BELOW
**Horsemen with a Grey and a Bay
in a Riding School**
*by Abraham van Calraet (c. 1642-1721).
Riding School manoeuvres were originally
training to ensure that a platoon of horses
could respond in formation on the
battlefield. Antoine de Pluvinel, unlike
some earlier teachers, disapproved of the
use of force in training.*

However, they are nothing new. They formed part of Roman cavalry training and were performed in French cavalry schools – but it is in the circus that they have been most widely seen.

The modern circus had its origins in England in the riding displays put on by Philip Astley in London in 1768. Astley had realized that when galloping in a circle, the centrifugal force made it easier to maintain balance when standing on a horse's back. He opened the Amphitheatre at Lambeth south of the Thames. This consisted of a circular arena with a proscenium framing a scenic stage. He engaged clowns and other performers and included dramatic pieces

LEFT
Poppy Jeanette
by Gilbert Holiday (1879-1937).
Modern dressage requires the horse to perform particular paces, steps and movements and to proceed in a variety of figures on the ground within rigid parameters of space. These include the pirouette, in which the horse keeps its hind legs over the same spot but turns a full circle around it with the forelegs, the piaffe, which is a trot on the spot, and the passage, in which diagonal pairs of legs are alternately raised and put down with a prolonged suspension between each stride. It must learn to make turns on both fore- and hindquarters, to move sideways and backwards and to proceed in diagonals.

BELOW
The Spanish Riding School
by Vincent Haddelsey (b.1934).
The showy 'Airs Above the Ground', artificial leaps and rearing positions are no longer part of modern Olympic dressage, but are still performed by the Spanish Riding School in Vienna, whose traditions go back to the sixteenth century, and the Cadre Noir of Saumur, the French Cavalry School. Here the horse is performing the levade; if this position is used to make forward jumps, it become the courbette.

RIGHT
Poster advertising the 'New Circus' in Paris in 1889. Circus tradition preserves many of the manoeuvres of haute école, such as this leap – the capriole, another of the 'airs above the ground'.

BELOW
The Circus
by Jerzy Marek
(twentieth-century artist).

featuring equestrian incidents. In fact, in the theatre generally, horse dramas became popular in the nineteenth century, especially the melodrama *Mazeppa*, in which the hero is tied to the back of a horse which gallops for two days and nights.

In 1772 Astley performed before the king of France and his court, and ten years later opened an amphitheatre in Paris. He went on to build another 17 permanent circuses elsewhere. In America John Bill Ricketts, a rider who had already appeared in Britain, opened the first circuses at Philadelphia and New York in 1793.

Circus equestrianism usually consisted of bareback acrobatics and gymnastics, but Astley's successor, Andrew Ducrow, was celebrated both for his horsemanship and for the dramatic mimes that he performed on horseback. He offered a succession of different characters or short scenes,

such as 'The Tyrolean Shepherd and the Swiss Milkmaid'. This was performed with his wife, and showed the courtships, quarrels and reconciliation of a pair of young lovers. Another famous act, much copied by later performers, was 'The Courier of St. Petersburg'. In this, Ducrow rode with his feet astraddle two horses while other horses, carrying the flags of the countries

through which he was supposed to be riding, passed between his legs in the opposite direction.

As the travelling circus developed with a mixture of clowns, animal acts, acrobats, knife throwers and other stunts, horses remained a fundamental feature. As well as acrobatics on the horse's back, equestrian acts might include 'voltige' (vaulting on and off the moving horse from different

demonstrates the enormous trust it
must have in its trainer. In such acts
the horse may wear protection, not
because the animal rider cannot be
trusted, but because of the risk of its
slipping, when it might unwittingly
claw the horse in trying to regain its
balance. Some circus owners would
exclude this kind of act for fear of
there still being an element of danger
for the horse. Indeed, the exploitation
of animals for entertainment and fears
that unscrupulous trainers might use
cruelty and coercion to create their
acts have turned some people against
circuses. However, though their case is
sound where wild animals are
concerned, they should remember that
the horse is a domestic animal and
asked to do the same sort of actions as
are carried out by a riding horse and
in dressage.

directions), forming human pyramids
with other riders on one or across
several mounts and spectacular forms
of dressage. 'Liberty horses' were
trained to perform complex routines
without riders.

In the huge three-ring circuses of
Barnum and Bailey horses were
exhibited in great numbers – in 1897
they were advertising a parade of 400
Thoroughbreds. As many as 70 horses
might perform in a single ring at the
same time; a poster of 1903 shows
three circles trotting in different
directions around horses which have
mounted plinths and rostra topped by
their mounted trainer at the highest
point. At one time the three-rings were
surrounded by an outer track for 'The
Great Roman Hippodrome Races',
presenting novelty races, steeplechases
and chariot races.

Sometimes acts combined horses
with other animals. The Soviet trainer
Irena Bugrimova and English Mary
Chipperfield developed acts in which
a horse allowed a lion to ride upon its
back, and Harry Velli presented a
horse-riding tiger with the Dutch
Strassburger Circus. For a horse to
allow a large animal that is its natural
predator to leap onto its back ,

The Hunter and Sports Horse

Ancient hunter and gatherer peoples stalked their prey or waited in ambush on foot; then, the horse was among the hunted. When people had learned to master the horse they could ride more swiftly after their quarry. At first, hunting was for food and to eliminate predators that could kill villagers or their livestock or animals that ate their crops. Later, when rank and occupation separated people, the mounted rider may not have needed to hunt for food. He rode out, perhaps to feed and protect the community, but increasingly as sport. Later still, hunting often became the prerogative of the aristocratic and wealthy, prohibited to others. Its becoming a pastime of the nobility has ensured that there are images that record every kind of hunting scene.

Hunting large animals offered a chance to display some of the courage and skill demanded on the battlefield, making a fitting recreation for a 'hero'. Like war, hunting could be savage and bloody. In one hunt alone the Assyrian King Assurbanipal II, hunting from his chariot or giving the *coup de grace* on foot, claimed to have killed 450 lions, 390 wild cattle, 200 ostriches and 30 elephants. The claim may be an exaggeration or include animals killed by others for him, but huge slaughters did take place. These were not animals hunted freely in the wild, but creatures bred or brought to huge game parks where they were kept for royal hunts and driven towards the hunters' arrows and spears.

The ancient Greeks probably had their hunting preserves, too, but did not have artificially stocked parks.

They honoured a skilled hunter as much as a victor at the Olympic Games. The Roman Arrian wrote the first known book on hunting in the third century AD, 'Give me young men who are not over stout,' he said, 'for the hunger must mount the noble horse amid the rocks, anon must leap a ditch.'

In the reign of the ninth-century Saxon King Alfred (the Great), hunting became the favourite sport of the nobility in Britain, but it was under the Danish King Canute that laws established royal preserves where hunting by unauthorized persons was punishable by death. In continental Europe hunting had already become

ABOVE
Rajput Princes Hunting,
an illustration from a Moghul Indian manuscript book of the mid-seventeenth century. The Moghul rulers of India inherited the horsemanship and archery skills of their Mongol ancestors, applying them to hunting as well as to war.

the prerogative of the nobility under the law of King Dagobert of the Franks.

All kinds of animals were hunted; in Europe everything from wolves and wild boars to wildcats. However, in both Europe and Asia, it was fleet-footed animals, such as the deer and gazelle, which became the favourite quarry. Alternatively, people also enjoyed hunting smaller animals and birds on which the falconer could set their hawks.

The art of hunting – venery – became strictly codified both in practice and behaviour. As practised in the French style it remains so, with 72 different horn signals just for a deer's movements. The French king who later became St. Louis wrote a poem 600 lines long on the proper way to hunt a stag.

58

Frederick, Prince of Wales, Out Stag Hunting
by John Wooton (c. 1682-1764)
and William Hogarth (1697-1764).
George II thought his eldest son 'the greatest ass and the greatest liar, the greatest canaille and the greatest beast in the whose world' and his mother called him 'a nauseous little beast', so it was perhaps just as well he died before his father and the succession passed directly to George III. However, a royal painting would have increased the fashionability of the painters. Wooton was a landscape and sporting painter who made a speciality of horses. Hogarth probably painted the figures.

OVERLEAF
The Grosvenor Hunt, Eaton
by George Stubbs (1724-1806).
This painting depicts the final moments of the hunt as the hounds close in. Hunting became a form of country exercise and a spectator sport with little to do with providing meat for the table. In the next hundred years, as the fox became the chief quarry for British hunters, this became even more true. As Oscar Wilde made one of his characters describe it: 'The English country gentleman galloping after a fox – the unspeakable in full pursuit of the uneatable.'

RIGHT
The Hunt
by Ferdinand Bol (1616-80).
A pupil of Rembrandt painted this scene which shows that noblewomen were as eager to follow the hunt as men.

As forest clearance in Britain reduced the availability of deer and similar quarry, hunting began to focus on the fox. Oscar Wilde made one of his characters describe a country gentleman fox hunting as 'the unspeakable in full pursuit of the uneatable', but stocking the larder had long ceased to be an important side of hunting. Concern at the disappearance of some hunted species and a reappraisal of human-animal rights has seen growing opposition to blood sports, but there can no questioning the influence of hunting on horse breeding.

The Hunter varies in type depending on the kind of quarry and the terrain to be hunted. All need stamina, intelligence, an ability to jump and to cope with the constant problems of travelling across country. In rough or hilly country a tougher, handy Cob type may be preferable, but a fast horse will be preferred in grassy country, and a Thoroughbred or near Thoroughbred is usually considered the best. The Hunter often turns out to be a good show jumper and the Jumper is now a recognized subdivision of the type.

Show jumping is a relatively recent sport, first featured at a Horse Show in Dublin in 1864 with three separate events in which horses had to clear a high jump of gorse and poles, hurdles and a stone wall. Such events gained popularity in Europe and first featured in the Olympic Games in 1912. After World War II show jumping became a major international spectator sport, with television attracting enthusiastic support well beyond the usual horse world.

Even more closely related to the hunting field is the cross-country race or point-to-point, which presents the rider with many of the same obstacles and stresses. Show jumping and the endurance test of the cross-country, combined with dressage, form the three-day event, which had its origins in the combined training of cavalry officers – hence its other name, the 'Military'. The first contest in its modern form was in Paris in 1902. The Championnat du Cheval d'Armes

(Cavalry Horse Championship) lasted only two days; the three-day form was established for the 1912 Olympics. It remained primarily a competition between cavalry men until after World War II.

There are many other equestrian sports. Polo is of very ancient origin. It may have originated in Persia long before the Christian era, and was played in India and China. It is said

that Crusaders took the game back to France in the twelfth or thirteenth century, but the modern game was introduced to Europe little more than a century ago. It had been played by British planters in Assam and then by the army officers in India, who took it back to England; the first full-scale match there was played in 1871.

Medieval tilting exercises, in which knights practised their charges aiming

ABOVE

Hunter with Master Up

by Henry Barraud (1811-74).
A typical mid-nineteenth-century country gentleman, Master of the local pack, surveys the territory over which they hunted.

ABOVE

The Game of Polo as painted by a mid-seventeenth-century Moghul artist. Polo probably originated in Persia long before the birth of Christ, and was a popular sport in China and Mongolia until recent times. In India it was discovered and taken up by British tea-planters in Assam in the 1850s and taken back to Britain by British regiments when they returned home. Thence it spread to North America and elsewhere. Argentina is now the country with the most polo players, and breeds most of today's polo ponies. A polo mount needs to stand 15 hands high or a little more hands high, so technically these are horses not ponies.

a lance at a target spinning on a post, are echoed in the Russian game of Kabachi in which the rider has to throw a spear through a ring. In Ethiopia the Gougs Game is reminiscent of a medieval joust, and in Argentina Pato is a kind of mounted basketball (originally the ball was a duck sewn up in a leather bag); Russian Sjurpapach, which uses a stuffed sheepskin hat, is similar.

In Afghanistan the ancient sport of Buzkashi is still played; riders fight their way through their competitors to snatch up a heavy goatskin filled with sand from a marked circle, ride away with it around a marker post and throw it back into the ring. Another Asiatic Russian game involves riders trying to snatch the largest number of caps off their rivals' heads – without, of course, losing their own.

Mongols have a very ancient-sounding sport, the Kouko or 'bride-hunt'; young men ride after girls and try to kiss them – not easy when the girls lay on with whips to keep them at a distance.

Each of these games makes its own demands for horses with speed manoeuvrability and obedience to the rider.

ABOVE
**Count Bathyany's Favourite Hunters
at Melton Mowbray**
by John E. Ferneley (1781-1860).

The Racehorse

Horse racing probably goes back to the earliest chariots and the first riders. Chariot races were part of the funeral games of Homeric heroes and were an important feature of the Olympic Games nearly 2,700 years ago. They were joined by jockey races in 648 BC. The chariot race was also a great Roman spectacle. The chariots started in an oblique line, like modern athletes in a stadium, and the competition was over seven circuits. In the first mounted races each rider had two mounts, leaping mid-race from one to the other.

As horse races were associated with pagan festivals and rituals, the early Christian Church condemned them. Under an edict of the Council of Arles in 314, the Church withheld communion from anyone who took part. Such prohibitions could not overcome the popularity of the sport and they did not survive, although in England under the Commonwealth, horseracing was banned in 1654.

The excitement of the horserace appealed to kings, princes and popes alike. In twelfth-century London a regular race meeting was held at Smithfield, and on Whit Sunday, Richard I's knights competed over a three-mile course for a purse of £40 in gold. The medieval annual horserace in the Italian city of Siena, in which horses from each of its 17 districts compete around the Piazza del Campo for the prize of a banner – the Palio – still generates the same fierce competition and draws spectators from all over the world.

It was in England that racing was established with the greatest status. There, too, the Thoroughbred, the breed synonymous with the racehorse,

Hambletonian', Rubbing Down (detail)
by George Stubbs (1724-1806).
This painting, made in 1799, of a
champion after a race in which it had been
heavily whipped and savagely goaded with
the spurs, shows the strain and
exhaustion of its victory.

Flora Temple and Lancet,
a Currier and Ives lithograph of a 1856,
shows a competition on Centerville
Course, Long Island, for a $2000 prize
given for the best three of five 1-mile (1.6-
km) heats. Lancet (under the saddle) won
with times of 2 minutes 25.5 seconds and
2 minutes 28 seconds (twice).

A Greek bronze of a racehorse and a boy
jockey, dating from the fourth century BC.
Horse races were an important feature of
the Olympic Games and other athletic
festivals and funeral games. The opening
religious ceremonies where followed by a
grand procession, then a 14.5-kilometre
(9-mile) race, with sometimes as many as
40 four-horsed chariots competing.

T.337.

was created. There had been a royal stud at Tutbury from at least the early fourteenth century, but the story of the creation of the English racehorse probably begins about 1520. King Henry VIII, a great sportsman, imported horses from the Gonzago stables in Mantua. Later, horses came from Hungary, and before the end of the sixteenth century a trade treaty with the Turkish Empire allowed the direct import of Arabian and Turkish horses.

In 1603 King James VI of Scotland, who already had a taste for hunting, hawking and racing, ascended to the English throne as James I. Two years later, when hare-coursing near Newmarket, he took a fancy to that part of Suffolk and brought his court there for sporting breaks. With his encouragement, Scottish noblemen soon established racing there. In 1627 his son, Charles I, inaugurated spring and autumn race meetings at Newmarket, and in 1634 presented the first of the Gold Cups which are still competed for. Newmarket became the headquarters of the British 'turf'.

The Civil War and execution of Charles I left an administration set

RIGHT
The Godolphin Arabian
an engraving by G.T. Stubbs after his father George Stubbs' painting, published by the Stubbs in 1749. Although not painted from life, the painting includes the cat who shared the horse's stable and was his particular friend.

ABOVE
The Byerly Turk,
an engraving after a painting by John Wootton (c.1682-1764), published by Fores Ltd of Picadilly, London. One of the foundation sires of the Thoroughbred breed.

LEFT
The Darley Arabian
an engraving after a painting by John Wooton. The second of the Thoroughbred foundation sires in another of Fores popular sporting prints.

against racing. However, with the restoration of Charles II in 1660, an even greater enthusiast sat on the throne – a jockey himself. He is the only king to have ridden in and won a race at Newmarket – the Town Plate – which is still open to any resident of Newmarket. By this time, races were being held regularly on 12 different courses.

In 1683 a Captain Bryerly, involved in the Turkish siege of Vienna, came into possession of a Turkish stallion. He took it back to England, and to Ireland as his cavalry horse in 1690, and then put it to stud. In 1707 Thomas Darley, the British Consul in Aleppo, obtained a horse of Muniqui Arabian type and sent it to

England. These two stallions, the Bryerly Turk and the Darley Arabian, together with another, the Godolphin Arabian, which arrived in England in 1729, were bred onto the best of English racing mares. One or all can be found in the pedigree of all Thoroughbreds registered today.

Of these three stallions the Godolphin, with its tiny ears and thick neck, had a less impressive appearance than the other two. The Bey of Tunis had presented him to Louis XV of France, but his appearance did not suit the royal stables and he was acquired by an Englishman named Edward Coke, who took him to England. After Coke's death he was sold to Lord Godolphin in whose stud he stayed

until his death on Christmas Day 1753 at the age of 29!

At this time the studs of continental European rulers, following the example of Frederick the Great, were concentrating on producing the best cavalry horses for their armies, but British landowners concentrated on developing the ideal hunter, carriage horse and racehorse. The British Thoroughbred was to prove unbeatable on the track for more than a century.

The first races in colonial America were run in the main streets of the settlements of Maryland and Virginia. Later, narrow quarter-mile (400-metre) courses were cut through the virgin woodland, but the first formal track

was laid out on Long Island. By the
time of the War of Independence
horseracing and the breeding of
racehorses were well established.
George Washington and Thomas
Jefferson were among their supporters.

It was in the next century, some
time after the Civil War, that
American jockeys began to use the
modern crouching posture. This was
derided in Britain, where it was called
'the monkey on a stick' seat – but time
has proved its value and it is now
universal practice.

While Britain developed the
Thoroughbred, various trotting horses
were developed in other countries: the
Orlov at Count Orlov's stud outside
Moscow from about 1777, and the
Standardbred and the Saddlebred
(Kentucky Saddler) in America. Both
of these American horses came from
stock that includes both Thoroughbreds and Morgans (all of which stem
from one sire foaled in Massachusetts
in 1793). The Standardbred, smaller
than the Thoroughbred and
particularly adapted to trotter harness
racing, is now one of the world's most
influential breeds. France also
developed a trotter, an offshoot of the
Anglo-Norman breed, and trotting
races were first held in 1836 at
Cherbourg in France.

The difference between trotting
and the other races is in the horses'
gait. Although wild horses use the trot
only when moving between a walk
and gallop, the trotting horse has been
specially bred and trained to maintain
this gait and to raise it to a tempo of
about 50 kph (31 mph). A horse which
repeatedly breaks into a gallop,
maintains a gallop for more than 30

metres (100 feet) or uses it to improve its position or to pass the finishing post is disqualified.

Trotting is mainly a harness sport, using a light two-wheeled cart, a sulky, but in France some trotting races are ridden.

Most races are run on flat courses, but a challenge after a hunt dinner in Ireland in 1752 between two country gentlemen to be the first to ride to a distant steeple led to the first known 'steeplechase'. Riding in as straight a line as could be found and jumping over all the obstacles was a new form of race. A track was specially laid out at Bedford in 1810, and others followed, including the Aintree course where the Grand National takes place. Steeplechasing demands horses of strength and stamina. The many jumps and water features and the number of horses jostling for position on them can lead to falls and injuries.

French steeplechase courses tend to have easier obstacles than those in Britain and Ireland, as they are designed to test speed more than jumping. The Pardubice course in the Czech Republic is even more difficult than British and Irish courses and has even more serious accidents. For those who care for horses there must always be some nagging doubts about the running of these races, but they do generate enormous interest and excitement.

ABOVE
Going Out at Kempton
by Sir Alfred Munnings (1878-1959)

LEFT
The Jockey
by Henri de Toulouse-Lautrec
(1864-1901).
The artist grew up with a great love of
sport. It was two falls when riding which
caused the atrophying of his legs in
boyhood and stunted his growth, but this
did not inhibit an enthusiasm for the
racecourse and he got to know many
jockeys, trainers and owners. This
lithograph shows very clearly the jockey's
'seat' – not sitting at all, but standing in
the stirrup.

Racehorses Before the Start
by Edgar Degas (1834-1917).
Degas at first painted mainly portraits
and themes from classical history, but,
from the time he met Manet and became
one of the circle of Impressionists, he
turned to contemporary subjects, such as
his well-known scenes of ballet dancers,
working women – and racecourses.
However, despite the sense of the moment
captured in works such as this, his
pictures were carefully composed and
painted in his studio, not out of doors.

ABOVE
Races at Longchamps
by Edouard Manet (1832-83).
Unlike Degas, with whom he often
enjoyed visits to the races, Manet did take
up the Impressionists' practice of painting
out of doors. However, he cannot have set
up his easel here, right in front of the
finishing line of the Paris racecourse.
Longchamps was laid out in the Bois de
Boulogne and the inaugural race was run
there in 1857.

ABOVE
Japanese woodblock print
by Utagawa Kuniyoshi (1797-1861).
These anthropomorphic horses are a satire
on human behaviour for the Year of the
Horse in the oriental calendar.

Acknowledgements

All pictures courtesy of The Bridgeman Art
Library, London; except the following which
were supplied by
C.M. Dixon 9 bottom, E.T. Archive 70 top and
bottom, 71 top, Viewpoint Projects 3,11,13,14
bottom, 27, 51 top, 80.